Stories Plus

Readings and Activities for Language Skills

Ann Gianola

New Readers Press

Stories Plus: Readings and Activities for Language Skills
ISBN 1-56420-208-9
Copyright © 2000

New Readers Press
U.S. Publishing Division of Laubach Literacy International
1320 Jamesville Ave., Syracuse, New York 13210

Printed in the United States of America
9 8 7 6 5 4

Director of Acquisitions and Development: Christina Jagger
Developmental Editor: Paula Schlusberg
Production Director: Deborah Christiansen
Copy Editor: Judi Lauber
Senior Designer: Kimbrly Koennecke
Designer: Patricia Rapple
Cover Designer: Shelagh Clancy
Artist/Illustrator: Richard Harrington

Contents

■ **Lesson 1:** Pleased to Meet You 4

■ **Lesson 2:** Looking for Bargains 10

■ **Lesson 3:** Caffeine Dreams 16

■ **Lesson 4:** A Mean Boss 22

■ **Lesson 5:** Life on a Farm 28

■ **Lesson 6:** A Chef's Secrets 34

■ **Lesson 7:** Letters 40

■ **Lesson 8:** Money Problems 46

■ **Lesson 9:** His Back Hurts 52

■ **Lesson 10:** A Hot Day in the Summer 58

■ **Lesson 11:** Moving East 64

■ **Lesson 12:** The Great Outdoors 70

■ **Lesson 13:** Language Problem 76

■ **Lesson 14:** An Ocean Adventure 82

■ **Lesson 15:** No More Bugs! 88

Listening Exercise Prompts 94

Pleased to Meet You

Grace Warner is a nurse. She lives in a one-bedroom apartment in Chicago. Her apartment is on the second floor of a building on Maple Street. Grace likes her apartment. The neighborhood is safe. The building is clean. And the neighbors are very friendly.

Tom Ferris lives downstairs on the first floor. He is a salesman. Tom likes his apartment too. He also likes Grace. He thinks she is very beautiful. Every evening Tom looks out of his window and up at Grace's apartment. Sometimes Grace looks out of her window and down at Tom's apartment. They both say, "Good evening!"

Tonight Tom looks out of his window and sees Grace. He feels a little nervous. He says, "Hello! My name is Tom."

Grace answers, "Hello, Tom. I'm Grace. Pleased to meet you."

Then Tom asks Grace if she can have dinner with him at the Chinese restaurant on the corner. Grace smiles and says, "Yes, thank you. But I need to be home at ten o'clock. I have to get up very early for work."

Tom is very happy. This is a wonderful apartment.

▮▮▮ Answer the Questions

1. What is Grace's last name?

2. How many bedrooms does her apartment have?

3. What is the neighborhood like?

4. What are the neighbors like?

5. Does Tom live upstairs? What is his occupation?

6. Does Tom like Grace?

7. Where is the Chinese restaurant?

8. What time does Grace need to be home? Why?

▌▌▌ Complete the Sentences

apartment 8	dinner 6	friendly 2	3 restaurant
beautiful 5	early 7	nurse 4	window 1

1. Please open the _____. It's hot in here.

2. My neighbors are very _____ people.

3. She doesn't like that _____. The food is terrible.

4. George works in a hospital. He is a _____.

5. This dress is _____. How much is it?

6. We usually eat _____ at 6:00 in the evening.

7. I always get up _____ in the morning for work.

8. Do you live in a house or an _____?

▌▌▌ Matching: Antonyms

____ **1.** likes   **a.** upstairs

____ **2.** safe   **b.** relaxed

____ **3.** clean   **c.** ugly

____ **4.** friendly   **d.** dislikes

____ **5.** downstairs   **e.** dirty

____ **6.** beautiful   **f.** dangerous

____ **7.** nervous   **g.** unfriendly

Making Plans for Dinner

Practice the dialog with a partner.

Good evening!

Good evening! How are you?

Fine, thanks. My name is Tom.

Hi, Tom. My name is Grace. Pleased to meet you.

It's nice to meet you too. You live in this building, don't you?

Yes, I live on the second floor.

Say, would you like to go out for dinner tonight? There is a very good Chinese restaurant on the corner.

Yes, thank you. I'd like that very much.

That's great.

But I need to be home at ten o'clock. I have to get up early for work.

That's fine. I'll meet you in front of the building in fifteen minutes.

OK. I'll see you there.

▮▮▮ Underline the Word You Hear

1. Marie lives on the (first/fifth) floor.

2. Their apartment has one (bedroom/bathroom).

3. Peter's appointment is on March (second/seventh).

4. Are your neighbors (friendly/unfriendly)?

5. Gloria (likes/dislikes) her old bicycle.

6. The kitchen isn't (clean/green).

7. This is a very large (apartment/department).

8. The manager's office is (upstairs/downstairs).

▮▮▮ Underline the Correct Preposition

1. The Korean restaurant is (on/in) the corner.

2. Susanna needs to be home (in/at) 10:30.

3. Mr. Lopez lives (in/at) a two-bedroom apartment.

4. What time do you get up (to/for) work?

5. I like to walk (at/in) the evening.

6. My sister lives (in/on) Los Angeles.

7. Is the doctor's office (on/in) the fourth floor?

8. The teacher lives (at/on) Seventh Avenue.

▌▌▌ Discuss with a Partner

1. Do you live in a house or an apartment?

2. Do you live in a big city?

3. Do you know your neighbors? Where do they live?

4. What are their names? What are they like?

5. Do you like your neighborhood? Is it safe?

6. Are there any restaurants in your neighborhood?

7. What time do you usually eat dinner?

8. What time do you have to get up for work?

▌▌▌ Topics for Discussion or Writing

1. Grace is a nurse. Where does a nurse work? What responsibilities does a nurse have?

2. Imagine that you live in a new neighborhood and don't know your neighbors. How can you meet the people around you?

3. What do you see when you look out of a window at home? Do you see other people? What are they doing? What else do you see?

Looking for Bargains

Teresa Dominguez likes to shop, but she doesn't like to spend a lot of money. She is happy when she buys something on sale. Teresa likes a good bargain.

Sometimes Teresa hears about a big sale on TV or on the radio. She also looks at the ads in the newspaper and in her mailbox.

Today Teresa sees a big sign in a department store window. It says that athletic shoes are 50% off. She goes inside the store. The prices are very good. Athletic shoes were $90, and now they are $45. Teresa's son Alex plays football. He needs new athletic shoes.

Teresa buys Alex size 10 football shoes. She gives a check to the cashier.

Teresa brings the shoes home, and Alex is very happy. He says, "Thank you, Mom! These shoes are fantastic. Oh, I forgot. Basketball begins in one month. I need more shoes. Maybe you can find them on sale."

▮▮▮ Check Yes or No

Yes	No	
___	___	1. Teresa likes to shop.
___	___	2. She likes to spend a lot of money.
___	___	3. Teresa hears about sales on TV.
___	___	4. Today she sees a big sign in a window.
___	___	5. The sign says women's shoes are 50% off.
___	___	6. Athletic shoes were $90. Now they are $60.
___	___	7. Teresa's daughter plays football.
___	___	8. Teresa pays cash for the athletic shoes.
___	___	9. Alex is angry about the shoes.
___	___	10. Alex needs more shoes for basketball.

▪▪▪ Which Category Is It?

baseball	football	radio	soccer
basketball	husband	sign	son
daughter	newspaper	sister	TV

Sports	Family Members	Places for Ads
1. _____	1. _____	1. _____
2. _____	2. _____	2. _____
3. _____	3. _____	3. _____
4. _____	4. _____	4. _____

▪▪▪ Matching: Synonyms

____ 1. happy   a. cost

____ 2. athletic   b. at this moment

____ 3. big   c. a good price

____ 4. bargain   d. excellent

____ 5. begins   e. perhaps

____ 6. maybe   f. used for sports

____ 7. price   g. large

____ 8. now   h. glad

____ 9. fantastic   i. starts

A Customer and a Clerk

Practice the dialog with a partner.

May I help you?

Yes, please. I'm looking for athletic shoes.

For yourself?

No, for my son. He plays football.

What size shoe does he wear?

Size 10.

Is black OK?

Yes, black is fine.

Can he try them on?

No, he isn't here right now. He's at school.

Keep the receipt. If they don't fit, you can return them.

How much are they?

They're $45 plus tax.

Will you take a check?

Yes, that's fine.

OK. Here you are.

▮▮▮ Write the Price You Hear

1. shoes _____

2. jacket _____

3. socks _____

4. hat _____

5. dress _____

6. shorts _____

7. suit _____

8. earrings _____

9. pants _____

10. skirt _____

11. boots _____

12. pajamas _____

13. underwear _____

14. watch _____

▮▮▮ Underline the Correct Preposition

1. The athletic shoes are (in/on) the second floor.

2. There are some ads (in/on) the mailbox.

3. My brother always buys things (in/on) sale.

4. There is a big sign (in/on) the window.

5. Is there a cashier (in/on) this department?

6. Do you have these brown shoes (in/on) a size 7?

7. Basketball begins (in/on) one month.

8. There are a lot of bargains (in/on) this store.

9. We heard about the sale (in/on) the radio.

Shopping in a Department Store

What does Teresa find in the department store?

Examples:
- Does she find shoes? — Yes, she does.
- Does she find milk? — No, she doesn't.
- Does she find televisions? — Maybe.

1. hats
2. cosmetics
3. dresses
4. blouses
5. jewelry
6. hammers
7. books
8. toasters
9. pajamas
10. ties
11. jeans
12. medicine
13. stockings
14. grass
15. radios
16. underwear
17. spaghetti
18. microwaves
19. flowers
20. coats
21. baby clothes

Topics for Discussion or Writing

1. Do you like to shop? Where do you buy clothes? How are the prices? Do you ever find bargains?

2. Do you look at ads? Do you buy things when you see them, or do you wait for them to be on sale?

3. Do you or any family members play sports? Are special shoes necessary? Are they expensive?

Caffeine Dreams

Juana Perez drinks too much coffee. She drinks three cups after she gets up. She drinks two cups at work in the morning. She drinks another cup at lunch. And she drinks two cups every afternoon. Juana drinks eight cups of coffee a day!

At night, Juana can't sleep. Sometimes her eyes are open all night. Juana feels tired in the morning. She has a terrible headache. Then she makes a big pot of coffee.

Juana calls Dr. Brown and says, "Doctor, I can't sleep at night. I think that I need a prescription for sleeping pills."

"How many cups of coffee do you drink every day?" asks the doctor.

"Eight," answers Juana.

"You don't need sleeping pills," says the doctor. "You need to stop drinking so much coffee. Your problem is too much caffeine!"

Now Juana drinks one cup of coffee in the morning. She drinks water the rest of the day. Juana feels better now. She can sleep very well. And she is saving money. Coffee is expensive!

■■■ Check Yes or No

Yes　**No**

1. Juana drinks too much tea.

2. At first she drinks coffee at work.

3. At first she drinks a cup of coffee at lunch.

4. She has a stomachache in the morning.

5. Juana calls Dr. Black.

6. The doctor says she needs sleeping pills.

7. Juana's problem is too much caffeine.

8. Now Juana drinks soda during the day.

■■■ Which Category Is It?

bottle	cup	headache	sore throat
can	fever	milk	stomachache
coffee	glass	soda	water

Drinks

1. _____
2. _____
3. _____
4. _____

Drink Containers

1. _____
2. _____
3. _____
4. _____

Health Problems

1. _____
2. _____
3. _____
4. _____

■■■ Matching: Definitions

____ 1. cup

____ 2. work

____ 3. lunch

____ 4. eyes

____ 5. headache

____ 6. pot

____ 7. prescription

____ 8. pills

____ 9. bedtime

a. body parts for seeing

b. a container for cooking

c. a small drink container

d. job

e. meal at midday

f. medicine

g. time for sleep

h. a pain in the head

i. an order for medicine

Conversation with the Doctor

Practice the dialog with a partner.

Doctor, I feel terrible!

What's the matter?

I can't sleep at night. I can't close my eyes. I am very nervous. I think I need a prescription for sleeping pills.

How many cups of coffee do you drink every day?

Maybe seven or eight.

How many cans of soda do you drink?

At least two or three cans of cola.

You don't need a prescription.

Are you sure?

Yes! Your problem is too much caffeine! You have to stop drinking so much coffee and cola.

You're right, doctor. Oh, one more question.

Yes?

Is there a coffee machine in this building?

▮▮▮ Underline the Word You Hear

1. much	match	**8.** cafe	coffee
2. pills	peels	**9.** caps	cups
3. drank	drink	**10.** kitchen	chicken
4. pot	pat	**11.** tired	tried
5. walk	wake	**12.** said	says
6. many	money	**13.** now	new
7. waiter	water	**14.** wall	well

▮▮▮ Underline the Correct Word

1. I (drink/drinks) too much coffee.

2. Lucy always (get up/gets up) early.

3. My eyes (is/are) open all night.

4. (Do/Does) you drink orange juice for breakfast?

5. Kathy and Bill (feel/feels) tired this morning.

6. Miguel (is/are) saving $50 this month.

7. How many hours (do/does) he sleep at night?

8. Mr. Nguyen (have/has) a headache.

9. She (make/makes) a pot of coffee every morning.

▪▪▪ I Can't Sleep!

Juana can't sleep. What should she do?

Examples: • Should she take a warm bath?
Yes, she should.

• Should she think about work?
No, she shouldn't.

1. drink a glass of milk

2. read a book

3. watch a TV program

4. call a friend

5. write a letter

6. run around the block

7. make a pot of coffee

8. clean the house

9. listen to loud music

10. eat chocolate

▪▪▪ Topics for Discussion or Writing

1. Do you drink coffee? If so, how many cups of coffee do you drink every day? When do you drink it? If not, explain why you don't. What do you drink instead?

2. Coffee is very popular in the United States. Is there a coffee shop in your neighborhood? How much does a cup of coffee cost there? How much does coffee cost at the supermarket?

3. Are you careful about what you eat and drink? Do any foods or drinks affect your health?

A Mean Boss

Parvin Mousa doesn't like her job. She is a secretary for a large insurance company. The office is very busy, and Parvin works hard. She speaks to customers on the telephone and does a lot of paperwork. Parvin works full-time, Monday through Friday, from 8:00 A.M. to 5:00 P.M. Sometimes she goes to the office on Saturday.

Parvin's big problem is her boss. His name is Mr. Grim. He owns the insurance company. He is not a nice person. He is mean. He is always in a bad mood. When Parvin says, "Good morning, Mr. Grim!" Mr. Grim answers, "I am not paying you to talk. You have work to do. Now do it!"

No one in the office likes Mr. Grim.
Everyone is afraid of him. Parvin wants
to quit and look for another job. But she
can't right now. Her salary is good, and
she needs this job.

Parvin is 36 years old and single. She
has many bills to pay. She also supports
her mother. What can Parvin do?

▮▮▮ Answer the Questions

1. What is Parvin's occupation?

2. Does she work for a large telephone company?

3. What does Parvin do at work?

4. How many days a week does Parvin work?

5. What are her hours?

6. Is Mr. Grim a secretary?

7. Is Mr. Grim a nice person? What is he like?

8. Does everyone in the office like Mr. Grim?

9. How old is Parvin? Is she married?

10. Does she support her father?

Complete the Sentences

afraid	company	mean	sometimes
another	everyone	paperwork	supports
bad mood	full-time	quit	
bills	insurance	single	

1. Are you looking for a part-time or a _____ job?

2. He _____ his parents. He pays their rent each

month and takes care of their other _____.

3. She wants to _____ her job, but she can't.

4. You need to have _____ for your car.

5. The secretary has a lot of _____ to do.

6. Don't talk to Mother. She is in a _____.

7. My son is _____ of dogs. He cries if he sees one.

8. _____ I work on Sundays, but not usually.

9. Is the head of your _____ a man or a woman?

10. _____ in my office is nice. I'm very lucky.

11. This pencil is broken. Do you have _____ one?

12. Ali is _____. He doesn't want to get married.

13. She is a _____ person. Nobody likes her.

I Want a New Job

**Practice the dialog
with a partner.**

I don't like my job.

Why not?

My boss is in a bad mood every day.

Why don't you quit?

I can't. I need my salary. I have a lot of bills to pay.

Maybe you can look for another job.

That's a good idea. I need to start looking.

I hope you find something soon.

Matching: Definitions

___	**1.** full-time	**a.** unmarried
___	**2.** boss	**b.** forms and letters
___	**3.** company	**c.** supervisor
___	**4.** paperwork	**d.** scared
___	**5.** quit	**e.** resign, stop
___	**6.** single	**f.** 40 hours a week
___	**7.** afraid	**g.** business

▋▋▋ Underline the Days and Hours You Hear

1. Monday through Thursday		Sunday through Thursday
2. Saturday through Wednesday		Friday through Tuesday
3. Tuesday and Wednesday		Tuesday and Thursday
4. 8:00 to 5:00	8:30 to 5:00	8:15 to 5:00
5. 9:00 to 4:30	9:00 to 5:30	9:00 to 6:00
6. 11:00 to 7:00	11:00 to 7:30	11:30 to 7:15
7. 10:00 to 6:00	10:30 to 6:30	10:45 to 6:30

▋▋▋ Use *in, on,* or *at*

1. Pam works _____ a tall building downtown.

2. Eric doesn't need to work _____ Saturday.

3. What time do you have to be _____ work?

4. Her boss is always _____ a good mood.

5. Your daughter is _____ the telephone.

6. Maria works _____ home.

7. Is there a water fountain _____ this floor?

8. My neighbor doesn't like to work _____ night.

9. He wants to quit his job _____ six months.

■■■ Discuss with a Partner

1. Do you like your job? What do you do at work?

2. Do you work full-time or part-time?

3. Which days do you work? What are your hours?

4. Do you work weekends?

5. Do you like your boss?

6. Are people afraid of your boss?

7. Do you like your job, or do you want to quit?

8. Do you want to look for another job?

■■■ Topics for Discussion or Writing

1. Are you sometimes in a bad mood? Discuss a time when you were in a bad mood. Why were you in a bad mood? How did you get out of it?

2. Describe your boss. Is he or she a nice person? Do the other workers like him or her? Is it important to like the people you work with?

3. How do you look for a new job? Do you need a job to support yourself? Do you support other members of your family?

Life on a Farm

Trinh and An Nguyen live on a small farm in the country. They are farmers. In Vietnam, they were farmers too. Trinh, the wife, likes living on a farm. It is quiet. An, the husband, likes living on a farm too. He doesn't want to live in a crowded city with a lot of traffic and noise.

Trinh and An have many animals. They have 30 chickens, 11 pigs, 6 cows, and 2 horses. Trinh feeds and takes care of the animals every day.

Trinh and An also grow vegetables on their farm. They grow corn, onions, potatoes, carrots, and lettuce. An works outside all day.

Life on the farm is not easy. Trinh and An get up at 4:30 A.M. and begin work. In the evening they are very tired. Sometimes their daughter, Lan, calls from the city. She says, "Sell the farm! You can move to the city and buy eggs, milk, and vegetables at the supermarket."

But Trinh and An don't want to move. They are very happy living on the farm. They answer, "The air is clean here. The grass is green. And we don't like going to supermarkets!"

▌▌■ Check Yes or No

Yes No

_____ _____ **1.** Trinh and An are from Thailand.

_____ _____ **2.** They like living in the big city.

_____ _____ **3.** The country has a lot of traffic.

_____ _____ **4.** Trinh takes care of the animals.

_____ _____ **5.** An works inside all day.

_____ _____ **6.** Farm life isn't easy. They get very tired.

_____ _____ **7.** Trinh and An get up at 5:30 every morning.

_____ _____ **8.** Their son tells them to sell the farm.

▎▎■ Complete the Sentences

animals	feed	grow	takes care
daughter	grass	supermarket	

1. Don't forget to _____ the dog twice a day.

2. Anya has one _____ and two sons.

3. They water the _____ every day. It is very green.

4. We can't have any _____ in this apartment.

5. Do the farmers _____ many different vegetables?

6. Helen goes to the _____ once a week.

7. Jaime _____ of the children in the evening.

▎▎■ Matching: Antonyms

____ 1. quiet   **a.** inside

____ 2. happy   **b.** difficult

____ 3. easy   **c.** buy

____ 4. outside   **d.** evening, night

____ 5. tired   **e.** sad

____ 6. sell   **f.** dirty

____ 7. clean   **g.** noisy

____ 8. morning   **h.** energetic

▪▪▪ Complete the Story

cows	farm	noise	restaurants
dancing	like	quiet	retired
exciting	night	relative	years

Eva and Armando Diaz are from the Dominican Republic. They

lived there many _____ ago and worked on a farm.

They live in Miami now. They like Miami very much. Miami is very

_____. There is a lot of _____ and activity.

Eva and Armando are _____ now. They don't work

anymore. Eva and Armando like to go out at _____.

They eat in _____, and on Saturday night they go

_____ at a nightclub.

Sometimes a _____ in the Dominican Republic calls

on the telephone. "Come back to the _____," says

Armando's brother, Carlos. "You are old now. You need a

_____ life."

"No, thank you," answers Armando. "We _____ the

big city. We like supermarkets. And we don't like chickens,

_____, vegetables, green grass, or fresh air."

▮▮▮ Underline the Word You Hear

1. The farmer likes his (wife/life).

2. Mr. and Mrs. Yang work (inside/outside) all day.

3. Does (he/she) live in the city or the country?

4. They have (thirteen/thirty) chickens.

5. It (is/isn't) very quiet here. I want to move.

6. Their (daughter/daughters) (calls/call) every day.

7. Lily has (two/ten) horses.

8. Do they grow (potatoes/tomatoes) on the farm?

9. You can buy eggs (in/at) a supermarket.

▮▮▮ Write the Price You Hear

1. carrots _____

2. potatoes _____

3. mushrooms _____

4. spinach _____

5. cucumbers_____

6. tomatoes _____

7. asparagus_____

8. onions _____

9. lettuce _____

10. peas_____

11. corn _____

12. peppers _____

13. celery _____

14. cabbage_____

▌▌■ Two Farmers

What do you know about Trinh and An?

Examples: • Do they live in the country?
Yes, they do.
• Do they live in the city?
No, they don't.
• Do they have a son?
I don't know.

1. have a large farm
2. have a dog
3. grow fruit
4. get up at 5:00
5. have a daughter
6. take care of animals

7. like living on a farm
8. take care of children
9. work outside
10. feel tired in the evening
11. like supermarkets
12. want to move to the city

▌▌■ Topics for Discussion or Writing

1. Is farming hard work? Did you or any of your relatives ever live on a farm? If so, where was it? Describe it.

2. Do you like going to supermarkets? What do you buy there? Is the food there good? Is it fresh?

3. What time do you get up in the morning? Do you work inside or outside? Do you work hard? How do you feel in the evening?

A Chef's Secrets

Marcel Dupont is a chef. He works in a French restaurant on Plaza Boulevard downtown. The name of the restaurant is Les Fleurs. Marcel makes excellent food, and he likes his job.

Marcel and his staff prepare many different foods every day. Marcel cooks delicious chicken, beef, fish, and soups. His staff makes salads and vegetables. They also bake bread and make wonderful desserts.

Les Fleurs is very busy. It is expensive. Dinner for one person costs between $45 and $65. But the customers love Marcel's food. Some people ask Marcel for his recipes, but he doesn't tell them. All his recipes are secret.

There is only one person in the restaurant who is not happy with Marcel. That person is Pierre, the dishwasher. When Marcel cooks, there is always a big mess in the kitchen. Dirty pots, pans, dishes, spoons, and knives are everywhere.

Pierre doesn't like cleaning up after Marcel. He doesn't like standing over the sink and washing a lot of dishes. Pierre wants to be a chef too.

▮▮▮ Answer the Questions

1. What is Marcel's occupation?

2. Does he work in a Mexican restaurant?

3. Where is the restaurant? What is its name?

4. What kind of food does Marcel prepare?

5. Is the restaurant busy? Is the food expensive?

6. Does Marcel tell the customers his recipes?

7. Who is not happy with Marcel?

8. Does Pierre like cleaning up after Marcel?

9. What does Pierre want?

▌▌▌ Complete the Sentences

17 bakes	21 downtown	25 mess	29 sink
18 busy	22 evening	26 recipe	30 vegetables
19 chef	23 job	27 restaurant	
20 delicious	24 kitchen	28 secret	

1. My favorite _____ are peas and carrots.

2. There are a stove and refrigerator in the _____.

3. Kim eats dinner between 6:00 and 7:00 every _____.

4. I don't tell anyone my age. It's a _____.

5. This cafe is never _____. It's always slow.

6. Chang is unemployed. He is looking for a _____.

7. This soup is _____! May I have the recipe?

8. Angela _____ bread in the oven.

9. They work in a tall office building _____.

10. A _____ cooks food in a restaurant.

11. Tom eats in a _____ once a week.

12. Your bedroom is a _____! Please clean it.

13. Her _____ for apple pie is in the cookbook.

14. Put those dirty pots and pans in the _____.

The Chef Has a Secret

Practice the dialog with a partner.

Your soup is delicious!

Thank you very much.

What's in it?

Oh, a little of this and a little of that.

Please, tell me. How do you make it?

Some chicken. A few vegetables. That's all.

Here is a pencil and paper. Write down the recipe.

I'm sorry. I can't.

Why not?

It's a secret.

A secret? You mean you can't tell me?

Yes, it's a family secret. Sorry. I can't tell anyone.

I'm sorry too.

You'll have to come back to the restaurant to have some more.

▮▮▮ Write the Amount You Hear

1. _____   5. _____   9. _____

2. _____   6. _____   10. _____

3. _____   7. _____   11. _____

4. _____   8. _____   12. _____

▮▮▮ Write the Number for Each Price

1. twenty-seven dollars and eleven cents _____

2. thirty-one dollars and ninety cents _____

3. twelve dollars and twenty-five cents _____

4. forty-two dollars and fifteen cents _____

5. fifty-four dollars and sixty-seven cents _____

▮▮▮ Write the Price in Words

1. $51.45 _fifty-one dollars and forty-five cents_ _____

2. $29.14 _____

3. $36.80 _____

4. $43.77 _____

5. $15.68 _____

▌▌■ In the Kitchen

Which things does Marcel need in his kitchen?

Examples:
- Does he need a spoon?   Yes, he does.
- Does he need a mouse?   No, he doesn't.
- Does he need a cookbook?   Maybe.

1. a bowl	**8.** a sock	**15.** a pot
2. salt	**9.** a hat	**16.** a dishwasher
3. a carrot	**10.** a knife	**17.** a pan
4. a measuring cup	**11.** an egg	**18.** a fork
5. paper	**12.** a calculator	**19.** a stove
6. a blanket	**13.** a sink	**20.** a chicken
7. a stepladder	**14.** a bucket	**21.** yeast

▌▌■ Topics for Discussion or Writing

1. How often do you eat in restaurants? What is your favorite restaurant? What is it like there? What do you usually order?

2. Do you like to cook? Do you like to wash dishes? Do you have a favorite recipe? What is the recipe for? Is it a family recipe? Is it a secret?

Letters

Ernie Basco is a U.S. mail carrier. He likes his job very much. Every morning Ernie wakes up at 6:00. He gets dressed in a blue and gray uniform. Then Ernie goes to the post office at 7:00 A.M. He sorts mail for the customers in his area from 7:00 to 9:15.

Then Ernie gets into his mail truck. He drives to the neighborhood on his route and parks. He gets out of his truck and puts a heavy brown mailbag on his shoulder. He walks around and delivers letters and packages to houses and apartments. Ernie likes to walk. It is good exercise.

Ernie is a friendly person, and people are happy to see him. Mrs. Perez asks, "Do you have a check for me today, Ernie?" Mr. Wong says, "Ernie, please don't give me any bills."

Ernie has only two problems. The first problem is dogs. Dogs don't like Ernie. They bark at him. Sometimes they chase him. The second problem is the weather. Ernie doesn't like the winter when it is cold and rainy.

Ernie's job isn't perfect, but what job is?

Check Yes or No

Yes	No	
____	____	**1.** Ernie wears a blue and white uniform.
____	____	**2.** Ernie goes to the post office at 7:00.
____	____	**3.** He sorts the mail for two hours.
____	____	**4.** Ernie drives his truck from house to house.
____	____	**5.** Ernie likes to walk.
____	____	**6.** People are happy to see Ernie.
____	____	**7.** Sometimes Ernie chases dogs.
____	____	**8.** Ernie likes walking when it's cold and rainy.

▣▣▣ Which Category Is It?

31 bills	32 cloudy	33 foggy	36 postcards
birds	dogs	34 letters	37 sunny
cats	fish	35 packages	38 windy

Weather Words	**Pets**	**Things in the Mail**
1. _____	1. _____	1. _____
2. _____	2. _____	2. _____
3. _____	3. _____	3. _____
4. _____	4. _____	4. _____

▣▣▣ Matching: Definitions

____ **1.** salary 39

____ **2.** vacation 40

____ **3.** uniform 43

____ **4.** route

____ **5.** winter 44

____ **6.** shoulder

____ **7.** chase 45

____ **8.** bark 41

____ **9.** job 42

a. occupation, work

b. money from work

c. hurry after

d. noise a dog makes

e. time off from work

f. special work clothes

g. a part of the body

h. coldest season

i. direction of travel

■■■ Complete the Story

afternoon	check	month	postcard
bills	English	package	send
carrier	mail	pieces	sister

Zoya is waiting by the window for the mail _____ to

get to her house. She is expecting many _____ of mail

to arrive this _____. The first is a letter from her sister,

Luba, in Ukraine. Luba usually writes every week. Zoya misses her

_____ very much and likes to read about her family. The

second is her Social Security _____. Zoya receives

$635 every _____. The third is a _____

from her son, Boris. Boris is visiting New York, and he promised to

_____ her a picture of the Statue of Liberty. Zoya is also

expecting some _____, and she will have to pay them

soon. The final piece of _____ is a small

_____. Last week Zoya ordered a book from a catalog

to help her study _____. She hopes it arrives today.

▌▌■ Write the Time or Times You Hear

1. Come to the restaurant at _____ tonight.

2. Marco gets up at _____ each morning.

3. He goes to bed at _____ every night.

4. My class is from _____ to _____.

5. That TV show is on from _____ to _____.

6. Gary will finish work at _____ today.

7. I'll call you at _____ tomorrow morning.

8. Are you coming at _____ or at _____?

9. Teresa is at work from _____ to _____.

■▌■ Underline the Colors You Hear

1. black and gray   blue and gray   blue and black

2. gray and green   red and green   gray and red

3. yellow and brown   yellow and black   yellow and blue

4. purple and green   pink and green   purple and pink

5. orange and red   orange and brown   orange and gold

6. silver and gold   silver and green   purple and green

7. red and white   red and yellow   yellow and white

▎▎■ Uniforms

In which occupations do people wear uniforms?

Examples:
- Do *bus drivers* wear uniforms?
  Yes, they do.
- Do *teachers* wear uniforms?
  No, they don't.
- Do *nurses* wear uniforms?
  Sometimes.

1. hairdressers
2. secretaries
3. photographers
4. electricians
5. housekeepers
6. security guards

7. taxi drivers
8. police officers
9. engineers
10. pharmacists
11. carpenters
12. babysitters

13. lawyers
14. cashiers
15. students
16. cooks
17. doctors
18. plumbers

▎▎■ Topics for Discussion or Writing

1. Dogs and bad weather are problems for mail carriers. What is a problem you have in your job?

2. In some jobs, you need to talk to customers. Do you like to do that? Do you feel comfortable talking to other people at work?

3. What is your schedule at work? What time do you start work? Do you have any breaks?

Money Problems

Mike and Fiona McFadden have money problems. Mike works as a teller in a bank. Fiona is a receptionist in a small office. Their salaries are not high. They earn a little, but spend a lot. When they see something they want, they buy it. But they do not have a lot of cash. Mike and Fiona use credit cards. Mike and Fiona are extravagant. They buy expensive appliances. Fiona wears beautiful clothes. Mike has a new car. Every year Mike and Fiona take a vacation.

Mike and Fiona have many bills to pay. Every day more and more bills arrive in the mail. They can't pay them.

Every week people from credit card companies call. They tell Mike and Fiona to send money.

Mike asks the bank manager for a raise, but she says, "No." Fiona asks her supervisor for a higher salary, and he answers, "I'm sorry. Not this year."

Mike and Fiona need to stop spending money. They need to pay their bills. What can they do?

Answer the Questions

1. Why do Mike and Fiona have money problems?

2. What is Mike's occupation? What is Fiona's?

3. What do Mike and Fiona buy? Do they pay in cash?

4. Does Mike have an old car?

5. Do they take a vacation every year?

6. Can they pay their bills every month?

7. Will their supervisors pay them more money?

8. How often do people from credit card companies call? What do they say to Mike and Fiona?

Complete the Sentences

appliance	expensive	raise	teller
bills	extravagant	receptionist	vacation
cash	high	salary	
credit card	problems	spend	

1. Patricia is a _____ for an insurance company.

2. I pay my _____ on the first day of every month.

3. I'm going to the _____ store. I need a new stove.

4. Ivan's _____ is $1,200 a month.

5. Martha gave her deposit to the bank _____.

6. You _____ too much money. You need to save more.

7. Good news! Jack is getting a $50-a-week _____!

8. Tim spends too much money. He is very _____.

9. I can't take a _____ this year. I'm staying home.

10. Chris has two big _____: no money and no job.

11. The company president gets a very _____ salary.

12. I only have $3 in my wallet. I'll use a _____.

13. He only pays in _____. He never uses credit cards.

14. That car is too _____. I can't buy it.

Asking for a Raise

**Practice the dialog
with a partner.**

Good morning, Mr. Green. How are
you? It's a beautiful day, isn't it?

I'm very busy. What do you want?

I need to earn more money, Mr. Green.

May I have a raise?

Why?

I have a lot of bills to pay.

What kind of bills?

Well, I have to pay my rent and utilities every month.

Yes, and you earn more than enough for that.

I also have a new car, my wife shops every day, and
we need to pay for our last vacation to Las Vegas.

**You and your wife need to control your spending. That
is your real problem.**

Please, Mr. Green, may I *please* have a raise?

I'm sorry. Maybe next year.

▌▌▐ Underline the Verb You Hear

1.	have	has	7.	tell	tells
2.	spend	spends	8.	earn	earns
3.	want	wants	9.	see	sees
4.	work	works	10.	say	says
5.	take	takes	11.	call	calls
6.	pay	pays	12.	need	needs

▌▌▐ Underline the Correct Word

1. He has a lot of (many/money).

2. They always pay in (cash/cashes).

3. Frank uses credit (card/cards).

4. Elena is a clerk in a (bank/banking).

5. I have a (new/news) car.

6. Leo can pay (his/he's) medical bills.

7. We take a vacation (very/every) year.

8. Please call me (on/in) Saturday.

9. These (closet/clothes) are too expensive.

10. Her (salary/salaries) isn't very high.

▌▌▌ Discuss with a Partner

1. What is your occupation?

2. Do you ever spend more than you earn?

3. When do you pay your bills?

4. Do you have a credit card? Do you use it often?

5. Name some credit card companies.

6. Which appliances do you have in your home?

7. Where do you shop for clothes?

8. Do you take a vacation every year?

▌▌▌ Topics for Discussion or Writing

1. Some people have serious money problems. They spend more than they earn, and they can't pay their bills. What can such a person do?

2. Are you extravagant? Do you ever buy things that you don't need? What is something that you want, but don't actually need?

3. Sometimes it is necessary to ask for a raise. Is this easy or difficult to do? Discuss a time when you asked for a raise. What was the answer?

His Back Hurts

Sam Erickson is a truck driver. He drives a large truck around the city five days a week. Big boxes of fruit are inside the truck. Sam delivers the fruit to many supermarkets.

Sam likes his job very much. He works full-time. His work day starts very early. Sam gets up at 4:00 A.M. and begins driving his truck at 5:00 A.M. Sam's job is also very hard work.

Sometimes his back hurts from lifting the heavy boxes of fruit. A box of apples weighs 45 pounds. A box of bananas weighs 50 pounds. But a box of strawberries is light. It weighs only 20 pounds. Sam likes lifting strawberries.

Sam likes to relax on the weekends. He likes to rest his back. He also enjoys spending time with his family and friends. Sometimes he cooks hot dogs and hamburgers outside in his back yard. Hot dogs and hamburgers aren't heavy to lift. But if Sam eats a lot, sometimes his stomach hurts too.

■ ■ ■ Check Yes or No

Yes   No

_____ _____ **1.** Sam is a taxi driver.

_____ _____ **2.** He drives a small truck around the city.

_____ _____ **3.** Sam works full-time.

_____ _____ **4.** Sometimes his elbow hurts.

_____ _____ **5.** The boxes of fruit are heavy.

_____ _____ **6.** A box of bananas weighs 45 pounds.

_____ _____ **7.** Sam doesn't like lifting strawberries.

_____ _____ **8.** He lifts heavy boxes of fruit on the weekend.

_____ _____ **9.** Sam cooks in his front yard on the weekend.

_____ _____ **10.** His stomach sometimes hurts if he eats a lot.

▪▪▪ Which Category Is It?

airplane	back	neck	strawberry
apple	banana	orange	train
arm	car	stomach	truck

Body Part	Fruit	Transportation
1. _____	1. _____	1. _____
2. _____	2. _____	2. _____
3. _____	3. _____	3. _____
4. _____	4. _____	4. _____

▪▪▪ Underline the Word from the Story

1. Sam Erickson is a (bus/truck/taxi) driver.

2. He delivers big boxes of (vegetables/fruit/cereal).

3. Sam (gets up/eats/drives) at 4:00 A.M.

4. A (bag/box/bunch) of bananas weighs 50 pounds.

5. Sometimes Sam's (neck/knee/back) hurts.

6. He likes to relax on (Mondays/weekdays/weekends).

7. He cooks hot dogs (outside/inside/at work).

8. If Sam eats a lot, his (head/stomach/back) hurts.

■■■ Complete the Story

aisle	delivers	job	stomachache
calls	drugstore	medicine	tablets
cashier	eats	prescription	
customers	hurts	recommends	

Liang Wu is a pharmacist. He works at a _____

on 54th Street next to a hospital. Liang is very busy today. Many

customers need _____. Mrs. Park has a

_____ for antibiotics. Liang gives her the pills, and she

pays the _____. Mr. Meyer _____ up to

renew a prescription. Liang's assistant _____ the

medicine in the afternoon.

Sam Erickson also visits the drugstore. Sometimes Sam

_____ too much. His stomach _____. Sam

asks Liang what he can take for a _____. Liang

_____ some antacid _____. Sam finds them

on _____ six.

Liang likes his _____. He is happy when his

_____ feel better.

▌▌▌ Write the Weight You Hear

1. _____ pounds   7. _____ kilograms

2. _____ ounces   8. _____ grams

3. _____ pounds   9. _____ kilograms

4. _____ ounces   10. _____ grams

5. _____ pounds   11. _____ kilograms

6. _____ ounces   12. _____ grams

▌▌▌ Underline the Word You Hear

1. back   bone   body

2. knees   neck   nose

3. eyes   ankle   elbow

4. cheek   chin   chest

5. shin   skin   chin

6. arch   arm   ear

7. hand   heart   head

8. toe   thumb   tongue

9. face   feet   finger

10. throat   thigh   thumb

▌▌■ My Back Hurts!

Sam's back hurts. What should he do to feel better?

Examples: • Should he see a doctor?   Yes, he should.
             • Should he move a piano?   No, he shouldn't.

1. deliver a box of fruit
2. eat a hamburger
3. clean the garage
4. pick up a refrigerator
5. visit a chiropractor
6. take antacid tablets
7. relax
8. rest in bed
9. take aspirin
10. exercise
11. go dancing
12. get a massage

▌▌■ Topics for Discussion or Writing

1. What time do you get up in the morning? What time do you begin work? What are your duties at work? Do you ever have any pain from work?

2. What do you do on the weekends? Do you relax? Do you spend time with your family or friends? Do you ever cook outside? What do you like to cook?

3. Does your back or stomach ever hurt? Do you have any other health problems? Do you sometimes take medicine? What do you take?

A Hot Day in the Summer

It is summer and the temperature is 101 degrees. The weather is hot, humid, and sticky. Paul Swanson feels miserable. He is hot at work. He is hot in his car. He is hot at home.

Paul doesn't have air conditioning or a fan. He doesn't live near the beach. His apartment building doesn't have a swimming pool. But Paul has an idea. He goes to the store and buys a small plastic pool for $29.95. Then he returns home and puts the pool on the grass outside. Paul fills the pool with cool water from the hose. He sits down in the plastic pool in front of his apartment building.

Some of Paul's neighbors laugh at him. They think he is crazy. Other neighbors think that he is smart. Mr. Jones asks, "Can my dog and I sit next to you?" Mrs. Hopkins asks, "Where can I buy a pool like yours?"

Paul smiles. His idea is very good! Paul is not hot anymore. Maybe he can sit in his pool at work tomorrow. Do you think Paul's boss will like his idea?

Answer the Questions

1. What season is it? What is the weather like?

2. What is the temperature?

3. How does Paul feel?

4. Is he hot at work? Is he hot at home?

5. Does Paul live near the beach?

6. What does Paul buy at the store?

7. How much does he pay?

8. Where does Paul put the pool?

9. Do some neighbors think Paul is crazy?

▋▋▆ Underline the Word from the Story

1. It is (spring/summer/fall). The temperature is 101.

2. It is (hot/warm/cool) and humid.

3. Paul doesn't live near the (bus/beach/bay).

4. He (bites/buys/brings) a small pool at the store.

5. He puts the pool on the grass (outside/at work/inside).

6. Paul (fills/feels/falls) the pool with cool water.

7. Some neighbors think Paul is (crying/crazy/creative).

8. Mrs. Hopkins asks, "(How/When/Where) can I buy a pool?"

9. Will Paul's (boss/neighbor/wife) like his idea?

▋▋▆ Matching: Definitions

_____ 1. degree

_____ 2. miserable

_____ 3. laugh

_____ 4. pool

_____ 5. car

_____ 6. crazy

_____ 7. smart

a. a place to swim

b. an automobile

c. intelligent, clever

d. insane or foolish

e. very unhappy

f. a sound of happiness

g. a measure of temperature

It's Hot Today

Practice the dialog with a partner.

How is the weather today?

It's hot and humid.

What's the temperature?

It's 101 degrees.

Oh, that's very hot!

It makes me feel miserable.

Do you have air conditioning?

No, I don't.

Do you have a fan?

No, I don't.

Can you go to the beach?

No, I don't live near the beach.

Do you have a swimming pool?

No, I don't. There isn't a pool at my apartment

building. What can I do?

Well, do you have a bathtub?

Yes, I do.

OK. You can sit in your bathtub all day!

◼◻◼ Write the High and Low Temperatures You Hear

1. Dallas __80__ / __65__   7. Atlanta _____ / _____

2. Toronto _____ / _____   8. Juneau _____ / _____

3. Portland _____ / _____   9. San Diego _____ / _____

4. Denver _____ / _____   10. Vancouver _____ / _____

5. Memphis _____ / _____   11. Chicago _____ / _____

6. Santa Fe _____ / _____   12. Phoenix _____ / _____

◼◻◼ Underline the Correct Verb

1. The weather (isn't/doesn't/aren't) cold today.

2. I (doesn't/don't/does) feel hot now.

3. Mimi doesn't (lives/live/living) near the beach.

4. Frank and Sara (isn't/don't/aren't) live in Toronto.

5. It (has/is/does) hot inside the car.

6. Their apartment (don't/aren't/doesn't) have a pool.

7. The temperature (is/are/am) 65 degrees.

8. The neighbors (liking/likes/like) his idea.

9. The water (feel/feels/feeling) cool.

The Temperature Is 101 Degrees

It's very hot. Do you have any good ideas?

Examples:
- Is it a good idea to go swimming?
  Yes, it is.
- Is it a good idea to go jogging?
  No, it isn't.

1. use the air conditioner
2. stand next to a fire
3. turn on the fan
4. sit in the sun
5. put on a jacket
6. go to the beach
7. take a cool shower

8. drink a lot of water
9. take a hot bath
10. drink hot coffee
11. relax inside
12. eat ice cream
13. find some shade
14. play tennis

Topics for Discussion or Writing

1. Do you like hot weather? What do you do when it's hot? What can you do to stay cool?

2. Do you ever do something "crazy"? What crazy things do you do? How do other people react?

3. Are you comfortable at work? Is it sometimes too hot or too cold? If you are uncomfortable, can you make yourself more comfortable?

Moving East

Tanya Simon is from a small town in Arizona. She is moving to New York City now. Tanya is an attorney and has a new job in a large law office. She is happy that she has a job, but sad to leave her family and friends in Arizona. And she knows her life will be different in New York.

In Arizona, Tanya has a nice house with a backyard. In New York, Tanya will have a small apartment on the 19th floor of an old building. Her rent in Arizona is cheap, but in New York it will be very expensive. Her one-bedroom apartment will be $1,400 a month.

Arizona is warm in the winter. Tanya needs only a sweater or a light jacket. But winter is very cold in New York. Tanya will need a heavy coat, scarf, boots, and hat.

Tanya is driving alone from Arizona to New York. It's a long trip by car. It is about 2,500 miles. Tanya is driving for four and a half days.

A big truck from the moving company is bringing her furniture this week. Tanya hopes living in New York will be OK. If not, she will return to Arizona and look for another job.

▌▌■ Answer the Questions

1. Where is Tanya from? What is her occupation?

2. Is she happy to leave her family and friends?

3. Where will Tanya's apartment be in New York? How much will her rent be?

4. What will Tanya need to wear in New York in the winter? Why?

5. How long is her drive from Arizona to New York?

6. What is the moving company bringing this week?

▌▌▌ Which Category Is It?

bed	cold	hot	sweater
chair	cool	jacket	table
coat	dress	sofa	warm

Temperatures	Clothes	Furniture
1. _____	1. _____	1. _____
2. _____	2. _____	2. _____
3. _____	3. _____	3. _____
4. _____	4. _____	4. _____

▌▌▌ Underline the Word from the Story

1. Tanya is from a (small/large) town in Arizona.

2. She is (happy/sad) to leave her family in Arizona.

3. In Arizona, she has a nice house with a (backyard/view).

4. Her rent in New York will be (cheap/expensive).

5. She will have a (one-bedroom/two-bedroom) apartment.

6. The weather in Arizona is (warm/cold) in the winter.

7. In New York Tanya will need to wear a (light/heavy) coat.

8. Tanya is driving (alone/with a friend) to New York.

■■■ Complete the Story

apartment	company	home	return
backyard	drive	moving	trip
bedrooms	friends	place	truck
building	furniture	rent	

Roberto and his family are _____ to a new house this

weekend. Now they live in a small _____ in an old

_____ downtown. The _____ is cheap, but

his wife and daughters need a better _____ to live.

The new house has three _____. It is in a quiet

neighborhood. There is a nice _____ where the children

can play.

Roberto plans to move on Saturday. He needs to rent a

_____ to move the heavy _____. Roberto

can _____ the truck. The _____ to the new

house is only about four miles. He also has many _____

who want to help him. Roberto will _____ the truck to

the moving _____ on Sunday. Then he and his family

will be ready for their new _____.

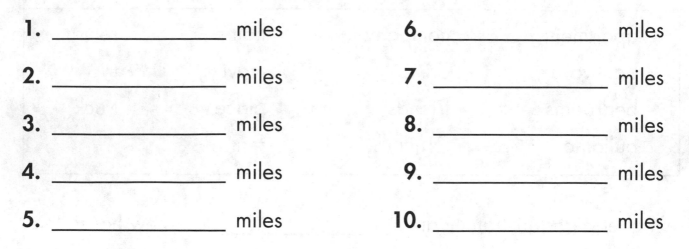

Write the Distance You Hear

1. _____ miles   6. _____ miles

2. _____ miles   7. _____ miles

3. _____ miles   8. _____ miles

4. _____ miles   9. _____ miles

5. _____ miles   10. _____ miles

Underline the Number You Hear

1. Emilio lives on the (fourth/fourteenth) floor.

2. Your appointment is on Monday, the (first/fifth).

3. Is the office on the (second/seventh) floor?

4. Katya lives on (Thirteenth/Thirtieth) Avenue.

5. This baby is her (second/sixth) child.

6. Can you come on the (twenty-first/twenty-fifth)?

7. My birthday is on the (tenth/twelfth).

8. The bus stops at (Eightieth/Eighteenth) Street.

9. English is his (first/third) language.

10. Kim is the (ninth/nineteenth) student from Korea.

11. Is there a flight on the (seventh/seventeenth)?

▎▎▆ Discuss with a Partner

1. Are you from a big city or a small town?

2. Do you have family and friends where you live?

3. Do you rent or own your home?

4. Do you have a backyard?

5. How many bedrooms do you have?

6. Do you have a lot of furniture?

7. Do you need a car where you live now?

8. How is the weather where you live now?

▎▎▆ Topics for Discussion or Writing

1. Is moving difficult? Where did you live before you came to this country? Where do you live now? How are the places different?

2. Do you live in a place that gets cold in the winter? Describe the kind of clothes you need to wear in the winter.

3. Do you enjoy long trips? Have you ever driven a long distance? Where did you travel? How long did it take? What did you see along the way?

The Great Outdoors

Brian Clark lives in a big city. He works in an office downtown. Brian sits at a desk all day. He needs more exercise. Brian thinks that hiking in the mountains is a good idea.

Brian goes to a sporting goods store. He tries on some clothes and equipment. He looks in the mirror. Brian feels healthy, strong, and handsome! He pays the cashier $325 for a new backpack, boots, hat, and sleeping bag.

Brian drives to the mountains after work on Friday. It is summer, and the temperature is 95 degrees. He gets out of the car and puts on his backpack and other equipment.

Brian walks uphill for 10 minutes. He feels very hot and tired. The backpack is heavy. He sees one snake and three lizards. Mosquitoes are buzzing everywhere.

Now Brian is not happy. He doesn't like hiking. He doesn't like exercise. Brian wants to go back to the big city. He wants to take off his backpack and his boots! He wants to sit in his office downtown and relax.

Answer the Questions

1. Does Brian work in a store?

2. Does he sit at a desk all day?

3. What does he think is a good idea?

4. How does Brian feel when he looks in the mirror?

5. Does Brian buy a new suit?

6. How much money does he spend at the store?

7. When does Brian drive up to the mountains?

8. How long does he walk? What does he see?

9. Does Brian like hiking? What does he want to do?

▪▪◼ Complete the Sentences

backpack	equipment	mirror	temperature
boots	exercise	mountains	weather

1. These _____ are too small. Is there a larger size?

2. In the spring, the _____ is usually cool and rainy.

3. Alex walks or rides a bicycle for _____.

4. There is a _____ over the sink in the bathroom.

5. It's warm today. The _____ is 70 degrees.

6. New hiking _____ is very expensive.

7. There are many wild animals up in the _____.

8. Fred carries his books in a small _____.

▪▪◼ Matching: Antonyms

____ 1. tired   **a.** downhill

____ 2. healthy   **b.** light

____ 3. strong   **c.** cold

____ 4. after   **d.** energetic

____ 5. hot   **e.** before

____ 6. heavy   **f.** sick

____ 7. uphill   **g.** weak

Two Friends on a Hike

Practice the dialog with a partner.

It's hot up here today!

Yes, it is. It feels like the temperature is a hundred degrees.

My backpack is very heavy. I need to sit down.

Good idea. Let's sit under that tree.

Do you like hiking?

No, I don't. My feet hurt, and I hate snakes and lizards.

And there are mosquitoes everywhere!

I want to go home.

Me too. I want to go back to the city.

Let's go back to the car.

There is only one problem.

What is it?

I forgot where I parked it!

▌▌▌ Underline the Word You Hear

1.	leaves	lives	**8.**	seats	sits
2.	store	stove	**9.**	pace	pays
3.	things	thinks	**10.**	boost	boots
4.	walks	wakes	**11.**	busy	buys
5.	doesn't	dozen	**12.**	snack	snake
6.	tree	three	**13.**	tried	tired
7.	big	bag	**14.**	hot	hat

▌▌▌ Underline the Correct Verb

1. Natalie doesn't (live/lives) in a big city.

2. The boots (is/are) expensive.

3. Sam usually (walk/walks) to work.

4. The weather (isn't/aren't) hot in the winter.

5. (Do/Does) Jessica sit at a desk all day?

6. Ruth and Jim always (drive/drives) to work.

7. These backpacks (feel/feels) heavy.

8. What (is/are) the temperature today?

9. My neighbor (work/works) in an office downtown.

A Two-Day Hike

You are hiking in the mountains. What do you need?

Examples:
- Do you need *a sleeping bag?*   Yes, I do.
- Do you need *a snake?*   No, I don't.
- Do you need *a tent?*   Maybe.

1. a rope
2. boots
3. a telephone
4. sunglasses
5. a backpack
6. a knife
7. a toaster
8. a jacket
9. a television
10. food
11. a hat
12. a sofa
13. an umbrella
14. jewelry
15. sunscreen
16. a map
17. a flashlight
18. a compass
19. a first-aid kit
20. water
21. insect repellent

Topics for Discussion or Writing

1. Do you think you need more exercise? If so, why? What kind of exercise do you like? What kind of exercise do you dislike?

2. Do you like to be outdoors? Do you live near any mountains? How can you get to the mountains? What can you do there? Where is another beautiful place to be outdoors?

Language Problem

Lev Platov is from Russia. He lives in the United States now. In Russia, Lev worked for a computer company. He was happy in his job. But he wanted to move to the United States. He wanted to live near his brother, Leonid.

Lev is looking for a job in Columbus, Ohio. Lev wants to work for another computer company. But Lev has one big problem. He doesn't speak English fluently. He needs to speak English very well before a company hires him.

Now Lev goes to a computer class every afternoon. He is learning about computers and computer terminology in English.

Lev also studies English Monday through Thursday in the evenings. It's difficult for him. Sometimes he feels nervous and unhappy. But Lev knows English is very important, so he works hard.

Lev wants to get a job by next year. He hopes to earn a good salary. Lev wants to buy a car and, in a few years, a house. Good luck, Lev!

▌▌ ▆ ▆ Answer the Questions

1. What is Lev's last name? Where is he from?

2. Was he happy in his job in Russia?

3. Why did he want to move to the United States?

4. Where is Lev looking for a job?

5. Does he want to work for a computer company?

6. Does Lev speak English fluently?

7. Where does Lev go every afternoon?

8. Does he study English in the evenings?

9. Is English easy for Lev?

▮▮▮ Which Category Is It?

Brazil	Chinese	India	Spanish
brother	England	mother	uncle
Canada	English	Russian	wife

Countries	Languages	Family Members
1. _____	1. _____	1. _____
2. _____	2. _____	2. _____
3. _____	3. _____	3. _____
4. _____	4. _____	4. _____

▮▮▮ Underline the Word from the Story

1. Lev worked in a (computer/commuter) company.

2. He wanted to live (next to/near/with) his brother.

3. Lev doesn't speak (English/Russian/Spanish) fluently.

4. He goes to computer class every (morning/afternoon).

5. He studies English Monday through (Tuesday/Thursday).

6. English is (easy/nervous/difficult) for him.

7. He wants to get a job (now/this year/next year).

8. He wants an American company to (fire/hire) him.

■■■ Complete the Story

car	difficult	language	office
city	fluently	manager	problem
computer	Japanese	nervous	salary

Elizabeth Cole works for a large Japanese bank in Seattle, Washington. She is a _____ programmer. She likes her job. Next year Elizabeth and the bank _____, Norimi Kano, are going to work at another _____ of the bank in Tokyo. Elizabeth will get a bigger _____ in Tokyo. But there is one big _____. Elizabeth doesn't speak any _____.

Norimi tells Elizabeth not to worry. She says that many Japanese people speak English _____. But Elizabeth still feels _____. What if life in Japan is very _____ for her? What if she can't learn the _____?

Norimi says, "Tokyo is a very exciting _____! You will like it. And there are many trains and buses. You don't need to buy a _____."

▌▌▌ Write the Day of the Week You Hear

Sunday	Tuesday	Thursday	Saturday
Monday	Wednesday	Friday	

1. The party is on _____.

2. _____ is his day off this week.

3. I am going to the supermarket on _____.

4. Please visit us on _____.

5. Do you study English _____ through _____?

6. The bank is closed every _____.

7. Her brother arrives on _____.

8. Jayne takes a ballet class every _____.

▌▌▌ Underline the Word You Hear

1. Russia   Russian

2. France   French

3. Portugal   Portuguese

4. Vietnam   Vietnamese

5. Sweden   Swedish

6. Germany   German

7. Japan   Japanese

8. Greece   Greek

9. England   English

10. Italy   Italian

11. Thailand   Thai

12. Spain   Spanish

Discuss with a Partner

1. Are you working now, or are you looking for a job?

2. Where do you want to work?

3. Is English important to you? Is it difficult?

4. When do you study English?

5. Do you take any other classes?

6. Do you speak another language fluently?

7. What do you want to buy in a few years?

Topics for Discussion or Writing

1. Learning a new language is very difficult for some people. Is it a big problem for you? What is especially difficult for you?

2. What advice can you give a person trying to learn a new language? Do you think going to a language class is helpful? Why or why not?

3. Lev wants to speak English very well so he can get a good job. Why do you want to speak English? Do you want to get a job in the U.S.? Will speaking English help you to get a better job?

An Ocean Adventure

Carolina Rico is a very rich woman. She has a lot of money. She has a big house, a large pool, beautiful clothes, and an expensive boat.

Today Carolina is sitting on her boat. She is sailing in the Pacific Ocean. The weather is sunny and warm. Carolina is very happy.

Carolina sees a small island and looks through her binoculars. A man is sitting alone on the island. He is waving a flag. The flag says, "Help!" Carolina sails her boat to the small island, and the man gets on the boat. He says, "Thank you! Now I can stop eating fish and coconuts every day! What can I do for you?"

Carolina says, "You can work at my big house. Can you keep my house clean?"

"Yes!" answers the man. "I am an excellent housekeeper."

"Can you cook?"

"Yes," answers the man. "I can cook very well."

"Good," says Carol. "I am very hungry now. Please get me some fish and coconuts."

■■■ Answer the Questions

1. Is Carolina rich or poor?

2. Does she have a boat?

3. Is she sailing in the Atlantic Ocean?

4. How is the weather? How does Carolina feel?

5. Where is the man? What is he waving?

6. Is he sad to see Carolina?

7. What can the man do?

8. Does Carolina give the man a job?

9. What does she want to eat now?

▌▌■ Complete the Sentences

binoculars	fish	island	rich
boat	flag	money	warm
clothes	housekeeper	ocean	
coconuts	hungry	pool	

1. The largest _____ is the Pacific.

2. Look through these _____. You can see far away.

3. I'm _____. Let's eat something.

4. Marta is a _____. She cleans rooms in a hotel.

5. Put the dirty _____ in the washing machine.

6. Their _____ is sailing in the Mediterranean Sea.

7. The U.S. _____ is red, white, and blue.

8. Many different _____ live in the Atlantic Ocean.

9. Hawaii is a large _____ in the Pacific Ocean.

10. It's 85 degrees today. It's very _____.

11. It's nice to swim in the _____ in our backyard.

12. Frank doesn't have a lot of _____ in the bank.

13. _____ are fruit that grow in the tropics.

14. Mrs. Lee is _____. She has ten million dollars.

◼◼◼ Complete the Story

coat	morning	salary	tired
job	old	shoes	walks
money	poor	small	

Sally Price isn't rich. She doesn't have a lot of _____.

In fact, she is _____. Sally lives in a _____

apartment on the second floor of an _____ building.

Sally's _____ is old. Her _____ are

dirty. She has a _____ in a factory, but her

_____ is low. She _____ to work every

_____. Sally is very _____ after work.

◼◼◼ Matching: Antonyms

____ **1.** rich   **a.** sad

____ **2.** happy   **b.** dirty

____ **3.** large   **c.** poor

____ **4.** expensive   **d.** old

____ **5.** new   **e.** small

____ **6.** clean   **f.** cheap

▮▮▮ Underline the Word You Hear

1. woman	women	8. berry	very
2. health	help	9. sailing	selling
3. tank	thank	10. walk	work
4. boat	boot	11. finish	fish
5. rich	reach	12. sitting	seating
6. though	through	13. small	smell
7. angry	hungry	14. closed	clothes

▮▮▮ Underline the Correct Word

1. The senator (is/are) a very rich (woman/women).

2. (Is/Are) this fish fresh?

3. There are two (man/men) sitting in the living room.

4. The children (am/are) hungry for their lunch.

5. Are (this/these) binoculars expensive?

6. Joe (is/are) waving the flag.

7. Vincent (don't/doesn't) have a lot of money.

8. Athena (cook/cooks) very (good/well).

9. Those women (have/has) a big house.

What Can You Do?

Tell about your skills. Tell what you can or can not do.

Examples: • Can you cook?   Yes, I can.
No, I can't.
No, but I can learn.

1. repair things
2. use a computer
3. cut hair
4. type
5. paint houses
6. take care of children
7. speak English
8. do construction
9. clean houses or offices
10. drive a car, bus, or taxi
11. play a musical instrument
12. operate a sewing machine

Topics for Discussion or Writing

1. You are alone on an island. What things do you need to survive for a long time?

2. Imagine that you are very rich. How do you want to spend your money? What would you buy? Why would you buy it?

3. Money can't buy everything. What are some things money can't buy? Does having a lot of money always make you happy?

No More Bugs!

Alfredo Leon doesn't like bugs. In the summer, bugs are everywhere! Alfredo is unhappy every summer. There are spiders in the bathroom. There are ants in the kitchen. There are bees in his flower garden. There are moths flying around the lights. There are flies on his food. And there are mosquitoes inside and outside trying to bite him.

When Alfredo sees a bug, he jumps up and screams. His wife says, "Don't be upset, Alfredo. Spiders and bees are good. They are important in nature. Don't be afraid. You are big, and they are very small."

But Alfredo doesn't care. He runs around the house with a newspaper in his hand. He slaps at every bug he sees. He is angry when a fly lands on his sandwich. He is angry when ants crawl inside his kitchen cabinets. And he is very angry when he sees a spider in the shower. Alfredo says, "Get out! This is my shower!" The bugs don't listen to Alfredo. They like his house, but not his newspaper!

▌▌▌ Answer the Questions

1. Does Alfredo like bugs?

2. When are bugs everywhere?

3. Where are the spiders? Where are the ants?

4. Where are the bees? Where are the flies?

5. What does Alfredo do when he sees a bug?

6. Is Alfredo's wife afraid of bugs?

7. Are the bugs bigger than Alfredo?

8. What is in Alfredo's hand?

9. What does Alfredo say to spiders in the shower?

Which Category Is It?

afraid	bathroom	happy	moths
angry	bedroom	kitchen	spiders
ants	bees	living room	upset

Emotions	Bugs	Rooms
1. _____	1. _____	1. _____
2. _____	2. _____	2. _____
3. _____	3. _____	3. _____
4. _____	4. _____	4. _____

Matching: Definitions

____ 1. kitchen

____ 2. everywhere

____ 3. scream

____ 4. sandwich

____ 5. shower

____ 6. newspaper

____ 7. bees

____ 8. angry

____ 9. spider

a. mad

b. something to read

c. insects that make honey

d. in all places

e. animal with eight legs

f. something to eat

g. room for cooking

h. a loud cry

i. place in the bathroom

Complete the Story

afraid	honey	sandwich	slap
angry	important	scientist	upset
bites	interested	screams	university
everywhere	newspaper		

Some people are _____ of bugs, but not Petra Black.

Petra is a _____ who studies bugs. She is an

entomologist. She works in a laboratory at a _____,

and she has bugs _____!

Petra never _____ when she sees a bug. She is never

_____, even if an ant crawls on her _____.

And she isn't unhappy if a mosquito _____ her. Petra is

_____ in every bug she sees.

Petra knows that many bugs are _____ in nature.

Bees make delicious _____. And spiders eat other bugs

that are not good. If Petra sees someone _____ a spider

with a newspaper, she feels _____. "Don't do that!" she

says. "Next time I will slap you with the _____!"

▪▪▪ Underline the Verb You Hear

1. like	likes	8. run	runs
2. jump	jumps	9. understand	understands
3. study	studies	10. make	makes
4. crawl	crawls	11. slap	slaps
5. pick up	picks up	12. scream	screams
6. listen	listens	13. fly	flies
7. bite	bites	14. see	sees

▪▪▪ Underline the Word You Hear

1. doesn't	don't	9. foot	food
2. his	he's	10. are	aren't
3. bathroom	bathrooms	11. very	every
4. everywhere	anywhere	12. science	scientist
5. garden	gardener	13. studies	student
6. bugs	bags	14. shower	flower
7. outside	inside	15. chicken	kitchen
8. angry	hungry	16. lands	lights

■■■ Bugs Everywhere

There is a spider in your shower. What do you do?

Example: I run.

I don't run. I put it outside.

1. hide
2. leave it alone
3. jump up and scream
4. cry
5. take a shower later
6. introduce myself
7. recommend a hotel

8. invite it to dinner
9. call 911
10. kill it
11. slap it with a newspaper
12. take it to a friend's house
13. spray insecticide
14. bring it to a scientist

■■■ Topics for Discussion or Writing

1. Are you afraid of bugs? Is anyone in your family afraid of bugs? How do they react?

2. What kinds of bugs are common where you live? What do they look like? Do they bite or sting?

3. Some people use insecticides to kill bugs. Do you use them around your house? Do you think they are safe? How else can you get rid of bugs?

Listening Exercise Prompts

Lesson 1
Underline the Word You Hear (page 8)
1. Marie lives on the fifth floor.
2. Their apartment has one bathroom.
3. Peter's appointment is on March seventh.
4. Are your neighbors friendly?
5. Gloria likes her old bicycle.
6. The kitchen isn't green.
7. This is a very large apartment.
8. The manager's office is upstairs.

Lesson 2
Write the Price You Hear (page 14)
1. The shoes are $37.99.
2. The jacket is $46.80.
3. The socks are $4.25.
4. The hat is $12.60.
5. The dress is $54.90.
6. The shorts are $11.34.
7. The suit is $149.08.
8. The earrings are $28.15.
9. The pants are $46.54.
10. The skirt is $17.82.
11. The boots are $83.59.
12. The pajamas are $21.53.
13. The underwear is $9.00.
14. The watch is $62.76.

Lesson 3
Underline the Word You Hear (page 20)

1. much	6. many	11. tired
2. pills	7. water	12. says
3. drink	8. coffee	13. now
4. pot	9. cups	14. well
5. walk	10. kitchen	

Lesson 4
Underline the Days and Hours You Hear (page 26)
1. Vincent works Sunday through Thursday.
2. Jean-Paul works Saturday through Wednesday.
3. Dan's days off are Tuesday and Wednesday.
4. I prefer to work 8:30 to 5:00.
5. Our office is open from 9:00 to 4:30.
6. Some employees work from 11:00 to 7:00.
7. Yesterday Jack worked from 10:30 to 6:30.

Lesson 5
Underline the Word You Hear (page 32)
1. The farmer likes his life.
2. Mr. and Mrs. Yang work inside all day.
3. Does she live in the city or the country?
4. They have thirty chickens.
5. It isn't very quiet here. I want to move.
6. Their daughters call every day.
7. Lily has two horses.
8. Do they grow tomatoes on the farm?
9. You can buy eggs at a supermarket.

Write the Price You Hear (page 32)
1. The carrots are 76 cents.
2. The potatoes are 82 cents.
3. The mushrooms are 1 dollar 78 cents.
4. The spinach is 42 cents.
5. The cucumbers are 65 cents.
6. The tomatoes are 1 dollar 19 cents.
7. The asparagus is 2 dollars and 21 cents.
8. The onions are 54 cents.
9. The lettuce is 85 cents.
10. The peas are 1 dollar 7 cents.
11. The corn is 98 cents.
12. The peppers are 2 dollars and 78 cents.
13. The celery is 89 cents.
14. The cabbage is 69 cents.

Lesson 6
Write the Amount You Hear (page 38)
1. The pizza is $8.99.
2. The taco is $2.19.
3. The cheeseburger is $3.85.
4. The sandwich is $3.35.
5. The shish kebab is $8.98.
6. The soup is $3.18.
7. The hot dog is $2.45.
8. The salad is $5.75.
9. The spaghetti is $6.00.
10. The teriyaki chicken is $10.97.
11. The vegetable curry is $9.99.
12. The ice cream is $1.75.

■ Lesson 7

Write the Time or Times You Hear (page 44)

1. Come to the restaurant at 6:45 tonight.
2. Marco gets up at 7:30 each morning.
3. He goes to bed at 10:00 every night.
4. My class is from 9:15 to 10:30.
5. That TV show is on from 4:00 to 4:30.
6. Gary will finish work at 5:40 today.
7. I'll call you at 11:20 tomorrow morning.
8. Are you coming at 7:00 or at 7:30?
9. Teresa is at work from 3:30 to 11:30.

Underline the Colors You Hear (page 44)

1. Tom is wearing a blue T-shirt and black jeans.
2. Ingrid has on a red sweater and a green dress.
3. Carol is wearing yellow socks and brown shoes.
4. The child has on a pink dress and a green jacket.
5. His shirt is orange with brown stripes.
6. Mr. Lee's tie is silver and green.
7. His uniform is red and white.

■ Lesson 8

Underline the Verb You Hear (page 50)

1. Hector has a good job.
2. Do they always spend a lot of money?
3. Elena wants a new car.
4. Does Ira work in a bank?
5. They usually take a vacation in August.
6. Do you pay your bills each month?
7. Tell Pat to pay the utility company.
8. She doesn't earn enough money to buy a house.
9. I see the manager at work every day.
10. They say that they don't have the money.
11. That person calls every week.
12. Mark and Kay need a new refrigerator.

■ Lesson 9

Write the Weight You Hear (page 56)

1. The bananas weigh 3 pounds.
2. The cherries weigh 11 ounces.
3. The pears weigh 2 pounds.
4. The apples weigh 15 ounces.
5. The melons weigh 6 pounds.
6. The strawberries weigh 14 ounces.
7. The pineapples weigh 2 kilograms.
8. The plums weigh 500 grams.
9. The grapefruits weigh 5 kilograms.
10. The oranges weigh 800 grams.

11. The peaches weigh 1½ kilograms.
12. The grapes weigh 400 grams.

Underline the Word You Hear (page 56)

1. Her back hurts.
2. My neck aches.
3. Amir has a sore elbow.
4. Grandfather has a cut on his chin.
5. I have a rash on my skin.
6. Their baby has an ear infection.
7. Does your hand hurt?
8. His toe is broken.
9. Is his finger swollen?
10. Charles has a sore throat.

■ Lesson 10

Write the High and Low Temperatures You Hear (page 62)

1. In Dallas the high temperature is 80 and the low is 65.
2. In Toronto the high temperature is 44 and the low is 36.
3. The high temperature in Portland is 58, and the low temperature is 49.
4. Denver's high temperature is 54, and the low is 37.
5. In Memphis the high is 86 and the low is 72.
6. The high in Santa Fe is 92, and the low is 81.
7. Atlanta's high today is 79, and the low is 63.
8. In Juneau the high temperature is 24 and the low is 7.
9. San Diego's high is 77, and the low is 60.
10. The high in Vancouver is 64, and the low is 56.
11. In Chicago the high temperature is 53 and the low is 38.
12. In Phoenix the high is 110 and the low is 89.

■ Lesson 11

Write the Distance You Hear (page 68)

1. 584 miles
2. 361 miles
3. 27 miles
4. 930 miles
5. 1,139 miles
6. 40 miles
7. 822 miles
8. 468 miles
9. 2,700 miles
10. 103 miles

Underline the Number You Hear (page 68)

1. Emilio lives on the fourteenth floor.
2. Your appointment is on Monday, the first.
3. Is the office on the seventh floor?

4. Katya lives on Thirtieth Avenue.
5. This baby is her second child.
6. Can you come on the twenty-fifth?
7. My birthday is on the tenth.
8. The bus stops at Eighteenth Street.
9. English is his third language.
10. Kim is the nineteenth student from Korea.
11. Is there a flight on the seventeenth?

Lesson 12

Underline the Word You Hear (page 74)

1. leaves	6. tree	11. busy
2. stove	7. big	12. snack
3. things	8. sits	13. tired
4. walks	9. pays	14. hot
5. dozen	10. boots	

Lesson 13

Write the Day of the Week You Hear (page 80)

1. The party is on Saturday.
2. Monday is his day off this week.
3. I am going to the supermarket on Friday.
4. Please visit us on Wednesday.
5. Do you study English Monday through Thursday?
6. The bank is closed every Sunday.
7. Her brother arrives on Tuesday.
8. Jayne takes a ballet class every Friday.

Underline the Word You Hear (page 80)

1. Svetlana speaks Russian.
2. Is Monique from France?
3. Portugal is next to Spain.
4. Is Vietnamese food very spicy?
5. Swedish is a difficult language.
6. Are they German?
7. I saw an interesting program about Japan.
8. This year she plans to visit Greece.
9. You need a book to help you study English.
10. Is there an Italian bakery nearby?
11. We saw their photos of Thailand.
12. He doesn't understand Spanish.

Lesson 14

Underline the Word You Hear (page 86)

1. The women are upstairs.
2. His grandmother is in good health.
3. Thank you for the ride home.
4. That boat is very small.

5. The rich man lives in an expensive house.
6. She attends class Monday through Friday.
7. Are you angry about something?
8. Is it very hot outside?
9. They are selling their house.
10. She never drives to work.
11. Do you like fish?
12. Ricardo is sitting on the patio.
13. I smell something cooking.
14. Her clothes are in the dryer.

Lesson 15

Underline the Verb You Hear (page 92)

1. Anthony doesn't like bugs.
2. Don't jump on the sofa!
3. My cousin studies English every day.
4. Ants crawl around the kitchen.
5. Please pick up a newspaper at the store.
6. Does she listen to the radio?
7. Mosquitoes bite in the summer.
8. Jeff runs for exercise every day.
9. He doesn't understand English.
10. Do the children make a lot of noise?
11. Freida slaps bugs with her magazine.
12. Don't scream! It's only a bee.
13. Airplanes fly over my apartment.
14. He is happy when he sees his brother.

Underline the Word You Hear (page 92)

1. Lucia doesn't sit outside in the summer.
2. He's afraid of dogs.
3. Where is the bathroom?
4. Close the door! Flies are everywhere!
5. Is the garden very large?
6. Adam is carrying two bags.
7. It's cool inside.
8. Don't be angry at your brother.
9. Is the food on the table?
10. Mr. and Mrs. Salim aren't here yet.
11. Is Mary very busy today?
12. My wife is a scientist.
13. Are you a student?
14. Put the flower in the living room.
15. Is there a window in the kitchen?
16. Turn off the lights when you leave.